NECESSARY LIGHT

May Swenson
Poetry Award Series

NECESSARY LIGHT

poems
by

Patricia Fargnoli

UTAH STATE UNIVERSITY PRESS
Logan, Utah 84322-7800

"At the Mystic Aquarium" first appeared in the *Cimarron Review* and is reprinted
here with the permission of the Board of Regents for Oklahoma State University,
holders of the copyright.

"Landscape in Blue and Bronze," and "Lightning Spreads Out Across the Water" are
reprinted from *Prairie Schooner* by permission of the University of Nebraska Press.
Copyright 1998 by the University of Nebraska Press.

Cover design and photograph by Barbara Yale-Read.

Library of Congress Cataloging-in-Publication Data

Fargnoli, Patricia.

Necessary light : poems / by Patricia Fargnoli.
p. cm. -- (May Swenson poetry award series)
ISBN 0-87421-276-6 (cloth)
ISBN 0-87421-284-7 (paper)
I. Title. II. Series.
PS3556.A7144 N43 1999
811'.54--dc21

99-6250
CIP

for my children:
Kenneth, Diana, Michael
and
my grandchildren:
Alycia, Joseph
and
for Roger

CONTENTS

FOREWORD

PATRICIA FARGNOLI, IN A POEM LATE IN THIS COLLECTION, IDENTIFIES herself (if I may take the liberty of assuming a correspondence between author and speaker) as being in the winter of her sixtieth year. Here, then, is a rarity that is close to an astonishment. For the authors of first books of poetry—and they are each year in the hundreds—are almost all young, and they have almost all of them risen through the same soil: workshops, MFA programs, initial life experiences. These beginning writers are skillful and hopeful; we are happy to praise their promise, their new voices, their energy. Ms. Fargnoli is another case altogether. She is, in personal and worldly matters if not in issues of publishing, altogether grown-up. She has been to the wars, and back. The dexterity and impress of her work, the fluency and clarity of her voice—which, to tell the truth, does not lack energy or tones of speaking I have not heard before—are grounded in rich and recognizable experiences. These are poems absolutely not of promise but of accomplishment. They are not so much about excitement and trial as they are about hindsight, wonder, regret, and rejoicing. They do not avoid the mean or the grievous, yet the note they strike most often is not of tribulation, but of a rugged gladness.

It makes sense, of course. Authority in poems is difficult to maintain if it does not come from the writer as well as the words. It is this force, invisible but in its place, that allows the formal construct of the poem to foster believability, and therefore import. And such authority is essential if the words are to carry us over the wild waste spaces of thought.

Altogether, the poem of experience (rather that the poem of idea) is the mainstay of this century's work. Such poems fall easily into two categories—some referring to experiences that are extreme, outrageous, and undoubtedly individual, and others to experiences that are usual and familiar: domesticity good and bad, marriage, mothering, work, the passage of time, the constraints of life as well as its resonance. The latter, I think, is the more difficult of the two categories, for when the experience is common, the task of elevation, of making that experience memorable, is all the poet's work, whereas if the experience to begin with is extreme or odd, an intensity has been achieved even before the scribbling begins. Indeed, transcribing and illuminating the usual patterns of life is surely among the most meaningful and the most difficult of our human labors.

I do not know how Pat Fargnoli came to her experience and knowledge. No matter how we try to delineate our lives, or are anyway willing to unveil our personal selves, there is a formality within art and a haziness within life that will not mix, and we end up not knowing very much. Neither do I know how she came to such an excellence of craft—except, probably, in the usual way, by the long and private labors: the hand holding the pen, the mind holding itself to the highest office. It takes—I trust you will believe me—a more than usual fortitude to labor well when one is youthful and full of energy, and how much more as the years accumulate, and other responsibilities enlarge themselves, and the body, that co-conspirator of the mind, must rest a little more, and a little more. It takes a perfect piety of devotion to excellence, to appear, not at 20 or 30 but at 60, with such an impressive, unflagging manuscript of relaxed and dancing poems.

Readers will discover many facets of Fargnoli's voice that I have not mentioned here, among them her affinity to landscape, especially her delicious containments of sky and sea; as well as her saucy and expansive humor, brightest perhaps in "Naming My Daughter" and "Visiting Frost's Grave." But I think the two attributes that will most impress readers are, first, the almost shimmering gladness with which she replies to the gifts of beauty and of human love; and, second, the compassion with which she addresses whatever is beyond her own intimate surroundings. Whatever it costs her, whatever it takes, there seems to be for Ms. Fargnoli only one world and only one way to live in it: with a ferocity of attention, care, and response. Central to these wonderful pages are the following lines:

> We go on. I don't know how sometimes.
> For a living, I listen eight hours a day to the voices
> of the anxious and the sad. I watch their beautiful faces
>
> for some sign that life is more than disaster—
> it is always there, the spirit behind the suffering,
> the small light that gathers the soul and holds it
>
> beyond the sacrifices of the body. Necessary light.
> I bend toward it and blow gently.

Mary Oliver

*I would like to step out of my heart
and go walking beneath the enormous sky*

Rainer Maria Rilke: "Lament" from *The Book of Hours*

*For among these winters there is one so endlessly winter
that only by wintering through it will the heart survive*

Rainer Maria Rilke: *The Sonnets to Orpheus* II, 13

ONE

HOW THIS POET THINKS

I don't think
like lawyers, quick in the mind,
rapid as a rat-a-tat-tat,
or academics, who pile logic up
like wood to get them through the winter.

I think the way someone listens
in a still place for the sound of quiet—
or the way my body sways
at the transition zone, back and forth
between field and woods—a witching stick—

or as though I were inhabiting the seasons
between winter and spring,
between summer and fall—
finding those in-between places
that need me to name them.

When I think, sometimes it is
like objects rushing through a tunnel,
and sometimes
it is like water in a well with dirt sides,
where the wetness is completely absorbed

and the ground rings with dampness,
becomes a changed thing.
Other times
it is the way sea fog rises off
the swelling green of the ocean
and covers everything but illuminates itself.

I think with my skin open like the frog
who takes in the rain by osmosis.
I delve into the groundhog holes
where no words follow.
Slow, so slow I think, and cannot hold
the thoughts except when they come down

hard on the paper where they are malleable,
can be shifted, worked at like clay.
I think like this: with my brain stem,
and with the site of emotions
the way I imagine the fox thinks,
trapped in his present need

but moving freely—his eyes quick
toward the day's desire—
and the way, beneath the surface
of the water, the swimmer's legs hang down
above the tendrils of the jelly fish
which wave in the filtered light.

I think in tortoise-time,
dream-time, limbic-time,
like a waterfall, a moth's wing,
like snow—that soundless, that white.

HOPPER'S PAINTINGS

The ones I like best are the ones with windows lit up:
"Rooms for Tourists," "House at Dusk."
In those there is a cool inner glow at least—
and with it hope of warmth, however insubstantial,
against the shadows of the night
which fall down over everything.
I can imagine the people inside of them,
solitary, yes, and yet not utterly lonely,
perhaps reading or passing slowly from room to room,
a hairbrush or toothpaste in their hand.
And the phone a silent instrument on the hall table—
a kind of peace emanating from the receiver
and from the light bulbs overhead
which are overloaded with silence.
The compartments of the houses are as enclosed
as the berths on an old Pullman
where, as a child, I rocked and rocked to the round
metal repetitions of the wheels,
not terribly concerned about where I was going,
the tunnel ahead, the rusted bridge we might pass over,
or the torn cities beyond it.

LANDSCAPE IN BLUE AND BRONZE

If she had lived, my mother would have told me
how my father wanted to hold her back from dying,
how he would if he could have, his arms
surrounding her all through her illness,

his hands, familiar as her own,
tracing the lines of her hips, the cord of spine—
wings brushing her inner thighs,
slow and insistent, committing her to memory.

She would have told how newborn
I burst from such touch, the way a conch shell
delivers itself from wave to sand, a life unspiraling.

Once in Guadeloupe I walked in the night
with a man from Majorca. He led me
out onto a dock that stretched into the Caribbean.

He didn't speak my language.
In silence we knelt
in the blue universe to watch fish shoaling,
their silver turned to bronze by the undersea pier lights.

Later in a white stucco room filled with gypsy music,
his hands were wings, his arms filled with light.
He showed me in most eloquent language
how love can be beautiful and brief—a fishtail
flashing away into darkness.

If my mother could return she would understand.
She would tell me all love is brief,
how memory can hold for a lifetime, how death

is like the sea where the fire-coral drops off
to bottomless canyon and bronze light deepens
to thickest blue and what waits there

is huge and tentacled—a reaching shadow.
She would tell me that nothing in the end
could have held her back
from swimming hard and fast away
toward the deepest water, its blue embrace.

FROM ELEVEN YEARS LATER

Even now I want to sit down
again with you on a sheltered beach
and hold your hand and burrow my fingers
through the black silk of your hair.
I want to speak with you in the round vowels
of your own language, to tell you how
I've named you *myth* and *memory*,
how I've made you a half-god.

In those days on the island, sensuous
with all manner of bloom
and the zephyrs off the Caribbean,
all the white rooms were filled
with night and lovers,
but I felt we were the only ones.

In your memory I know I am not
even a fragment, or if so,
it's not my brown eyes you recall
nor the hibiscus in my hair,
not my name, not the slope of my belly,
but only a shadow, one woman among many,
an American who clung to your knotted shoulders
each night for a week and was insatiable.

I want you to explain how the ecstasy
we so cruelly name *lust*
can come and go for you so easily.
Any woman would tell you
there should be another name. Love,
I want you to teach me again

the holy practices of my body,
how it bends, how it rises.
Lean your head against the hollow
of my throat. Kiss the small scar,
the blood-warm and animal pulse there.

BREAKING SILENCE—FOR MY SON

The night you were conceived
your father drove up Avon Mountain
and into the roadside rest
that looked over the little city,
its handful of scattered sparks.
I was eighteen and thin then
but the front seat of the 1956 Dodge
seemed cramped and dark,
the new diamond, I hadn't known
how to refuse, trapping flecks of light.
Even then the blackness was thick
as a muck you could swim through.
Your father pushed me down
on the scratchy seat, not roughly
but as if staking a claim,
and his face rose like
a thin-shadowed moon above me.
My legs ached in those peculiar angles,
my head bumped against the door.
I know you want me to say I loved him
but I wanted only to belong—to anyone.
So I let it happen,
the way I let all of it happen—
the marriage, his drinking, the rage.
This is not to say I loved you any less—
only I was young and didn't know yet
we can choose our lives.
It was dark in the car.
Such weight and pressure,
the wet earthy smell of night,
a slickness like glue.
And in a distant inviolate place,
as though it had nothing at all
to do with him, you were a spark
in silence catching.

NAMING MY DAUGHTER

In the Uruba tribe of Africa, children are
named not only at birth but throughout their
lives by their characteristics and the events
that befall them.

The one who took hold in the cold night
The one who kicked loudly
The one who slid down quickly in the ice storm
She who came while the doctor was eating dessert
New one held up by heels in the glare
The river between two brothers
Second pot on the stove
Princess of a hundred dolls
Hair like water falling beneath moonlight
Strides into the day
She who runs away with motorcycle club president
Daughter kicked with a boot
Daughter blizzard in the sky
Daughter night-pocket
She who sells sports club memberships
One who loves over and over
She who wants child but lost one.
She who wants marriage but has none
She who never gives up
Diana (Goddess of the Chase)
Doris (for the carrot-top grandmother
she never knew)
Fargnoli (for the father
who drank and left and died)
Peter Pan, Iron Pumper
Tumbleweed who goes months without calling
Daughter who is a pillar of light
Daughter mirror, Daughter stands alone
Daughter boomerang who always comes back
Daughter who flies forward into the day
where I will be nameless.

GOING

The children walk off
into crowds of strangers,
their laces are tied,
their backs straight.
They wave to you
from platforms you cannot reach.
You want to hang on.
Running after them,
you thrust out small packages:
vitamins, a new blouse, guilt.
But they keep discarding
your dreams for their own.
They carry your admonitions
in their pockets
and their children will sing
your lullabies,
so that, finally, knowing this,
you let go.
They blur, fade.
You settle back.
The years pass, silent as clouds.
Sundays, they come for dinner,
serve up slices of their lives,
but it's not the same.
Sometimes, in a crowd,
you will catch a glimpse
of long braids,
a ribbon streaming,
and you will remember—
a head beneath your hand,
a quilt tucked in,
small things snapping on a line.

MINIATURE

after Yannis Ritsos

She lifts slices of orange from the cutting board
and lays them overlapping
on a plate with blue flowers,
the asters that grow in profusion
by her roadside.
Leaned back into the swirl
of his smoke, he stares at the opposite wall
as if something has disturbed it
and he has no control.
A mechanical hum,
the only sound in the room
and that, soft, almost silent.
Something sad and unassailable
has drifted away from them
and will not return.
They pretend they did not see it go.
They pretend love is still possible,
the way asters cling to some diminished
version of blue long past their peak season.
They pretend their lives are an endless rolling
through the one moment they share here
and on to the next.

SEA WATCHERS

after Hopper

Their two faces match
the sand itself
as they sit on a bench
staring outward
toward the calm ocean
beyond the harsh angles
of the cottage,
the gray cement deck,
the dull green bench.
The sea looks as if
it will never move again.

A chain linking
two gray pilings
is as stiff as the frozen
rectangles of towels
on their line.
They have quarreled
or worse
they have not quarreled
but have arrived
at this stony place

from a long line
of grievances,
like beach trash heaped
higher and higher
until gulls, waves,
the wind haul it all
piece by piece away—
brack and kelp, shells,
the flesh of dead fish,
sand, bones.
Only twin jettys
of rock remain.

FROM A RENTED COTTAGE BY WINNISQUAM IN RAIN

In the Lake Region Hospital
someone I love is in danger, could be dying.
And because there is nothing else to be done,
I keep watch by writing
before a window pasted with old seeds
as the gray lake swallows the gray rain.

It is early evening
and the lake is tarnished silver
in the gradual disappearance of light.
In the shadows behind me, his shirt
is still flung on the chair back,
his toast crumbs still on the table.

The rain falls heavily from the eaves
like a song played over and over—a rhythm
that would slip anyone off to sleep.

Only I am not even tired
and I want the notes of the rain
to play like panpipes in the hidden places
where I think my soul lives.
I want them to take watery root there.

I believe I do have a soul—
else why, as I keep these long hours
alone before the dark glass,
do I begin to understand boundaries—

how near we all are to each other—
how near life is to death—
how near I am to rain—
how everything, sooner or later, crosses over.

He probably will be saved after all—
only something that's burst inside,
a small thing—non-essential and treatable.

And would you believe
that just now, beyond the window
and under the eaves,
in all the heavy downpouring—
in all the awful danger of drowning—
the smallest insect
darted up on its delicate gnat wings?

AT THE MYSTIC AQUARIUM

Still sun blind, I wheel your chair
through the darkened room
to the largest tank, where hammerheads swim
in the aquamarine glow, the torpedo of their bodies
sleeking past you beyond the glass.
Wanting respite from the heavy pushing,
wanting unburdened time to take in
the small brilliant lives of darting reef fish,
for once, I leave you, brake on and safe.

    But when I turn away into the milling crowd,
it is I who fall—only a few feet from you, tripping
over a small girl, my body old, heavy,
coming down on her, her arms flailing,
trying to fight it back.

    She lets out a cry that rips straight through
and her mother snatches her up, snaps at me in anger.
Sorry. Sorry. I say again and again
as I try with no luck to struggle to my feet,
straining against the dark and the gravity,
thinking how hard it is to rise
from the downthrust of weight and age,
aware of shame's bloodrush, tears beginning
as if I were the hurt child, the one who needed saving.

    Suddenly I hate your wheelchair,
the knees that will not hold you, your blocked heart.
I want you here at my elbow, your hand pulling me up,
your arm gripping my shoulder, comforts in my ear.

    But you've never even noticed, hooked as you are
to the aqua light, flashing points of the teeth,
the flat implacable eyes.

GIFTS

I bring you cobblestones from the cold sea,
from the seventh cove of Cranberry Island—
where the beach is not sand
but stones piled on stones.

What color? you ask, when you call
from your mountainside home far from the sea.
Gray, I tell you. *Blue, black, white,* I say.
I *mean* to say: washed gray of a fogged-in morning,

white of salt, of seafoam, night-black,
blue of a far harbor. I mean to say:
red of rust, red of dried seaweed, yellow-pale,
streaked with the first coral of dawn.

Because I wanted to bring them to you,
I weighed down my pockets as much as I dared
and walked back, light-souled and three pounds heavier,
up the grassy path from the sea to the cottage.

I wanted to bring them to you because they are
the shades of grief and of mourning,
they are patience, endurance—
the exact pigmentation of pain.

And don't we know about endurance?
And don't we know about pain?
Now I have spread them out on the wooden
kitchen table. Gently they click and clatter.

They are gathering their thick voices.
If we listen—will they teach us to sing?

EVENSONG

It is dusk, Roger, and already you
are sleeping on the pillowback couch, head
back, mouth barely open, gray hair in tufts.

Across the courtyard, the windows lighting
have nothing to do with us, and I curl
in the old vinyl chair, watching you sleep

and watching the nightclouds roll in over
the thin margin of woods that surrounds us.
In this unguarded moment, the deep lines

of your face are as relaxed as rivers
that have wandered beyond their boundaries,
even the small, tight muscles of your eyes

and lips softened, as though in sleep you had
let go of your history: the pills you've
swallowed; all those admissions.

Dear one, the time I have feared the most
has nearly come, and I write this poem in
tenderness and longing for all I cannot change:

the way your illness slowly takes your mind,
what manner of living is left to you,
the shadowed space my arms encircle each night.

How I have wanted to take all of our
fears in my arms and run with you while we
still can, back to those years when your room was

one flight up in a house on River Road,
my poem was on your wall and beyond your
shaded window there was no world.

THE SLEEPERS

In the orchard of horses
among statues of horses,
a man lies sleeping.
His clothes, no color
and torn. His beard and hair,
long and gray and salt-caked
as the curl of waves in winter.
The horses don't notice,
quiet as they are
in their bronze-green poses—
horses too small to carry him,
too tall for him to climb.
The woman comes softly in gauze
and red beads. She bends down
and lifts his huge head,
strong curve of jaw
heavy as marble. She holds him;
in the dark cavity of her chest,
a cardinal dives and soars,
wings, a small fire.
Suddenly she knows who he is.
She tries to tell the others
who are with her
in the orchard of horses,
in the kitchen of the poor.
Old woman at the stove, stirring
the soup with a dented tin spoon,
men in sweat-pants in the halls,
apple-pickers on their ladders,
heads lost among the gnarled branches.
But no one looks up.
If she wills him not to die,
can he keep sleeping?
She holds the reins
of his sleep, her dream.

Meanwhile the horses ride,
each in its own place,
out of the country of longing.

THE DECISION

It was autumn, and I sat at the kitchen table
making lists for yes and no
on the backs of envelopes.
                    Early evening
and already dark. The dog stretched out
by my feet, and I lifted my head
to stare out the window
where the interstate rushed and roared
                    —a great river.
  I rose and leaned my forehead against the glass.
Rain from the storm just past
shook in the leaves as the wind
                    swept through them.
When I was a child I would go out
in the fields and lie in the waist-high grasses,
imagine I rode rain over the horizon.

When you called, I sighed
and said *yes* and *yes* and *I know*,
                    but my heart
was already loading cartons, stacking them.
It had been raining on and off all day—
wavering lines in the gray mist, then
                    hard and straight.

NIGHTWORK

A blue tarp covers the opening the new owner has cut
in the roof of the brick house next door.
Up there all Saturday, balancing on the incline,
his saw affronting the neighborhood.
Tonight, the man works beneath it,

the tarp a blue glow in his torchlight.
From my second story apartment I can see
his silhouette, shoulders and head,
arm swinging out—a huge fish swimming
a tank—that aqua and silent.

Remember last summer—the aquarium?
In the darkened room, I pushed your wheelchair
close to the viewing glass. We watched hammerheads
slide past, circling, circling—their purpose:
to swim, swallow, give birth.

Love can be long and difficult: sixteen years,
crushed under your tirades, your inescapable pain.
Understand, I had to move away.

Next door the man is swimming alone
beneath his blue tarp. I hear the bell-bang
of his hammer; I hear a drill.
When someone moves in, they change a place,
bring something from behind, make something new.

I think my neighbor is constructing
more room, raising a dormer,
but I will miss the old roof line, watching the light
bounce off rusted tin,
hearing the wind lift torn shingles.

SAG HARBOR SUNDOWN

for Maureen Mecagni

Later that afternoon
after the windblown rolling
of the Cross Sound ferry,
after my nap in your spare spindle bed,
when the crows descended
into the scrub pine forest, the yawls
slunk silently back into the harbor
      and we sat on your wooden deck
talking of your work
for the Whaler's Presbyterian,
mine at the clinic; how we ache
in all the wrong places, clichés
about pounds gained, discovering gray.
      No talk of death—though these days
it always surrounds us—the shadow
of a cloud moving across water,
an answering shadow moving beneath waves.
      Instead, you told me how you leave
old bread, milk-soaked, in saucers
for the creatures that come
at night out of the scrub pines
and about last December's deer
running wounded to your lawn
where she stood motionless, a stone,
before bounding into the opposite forest—
the trail of her blood
bothering your days long afterward.
      As though no time had passed
we looked out over the sound
in that absent-minded way we've learned
to stare into the past or beyond the present.
We stayed there until night floated
a last sail across the ebbing water.

Far into the silver, the rolling hum carries me.
Top deck of the ferry, at the back rail, I watch
herring gulls ride updrafts, collapse on bread chunks
tossed by a small boy in an outsized tee shirt.
They whiten the gray with their noisy hungers.

Below, in the great room, others doze,
play set-back, queue up for coffee.
Leashed to a chair leg, a terrier starts yapping.
In the sting of the spray, I am aware
I am one of them, know I am not one of them,

know that beneath the waves' patina,
the unseen slides by in silvery shadows.
I understand hunger—
why the shearwater grazes the whitecaps.
I know that, behind me, the wake
stretches shining—a road I can't follow.

The rail I lean on beads with silver.
My breath is a mist, warm, heavy with brine.
Silver everywhere, evening on the rim.
Nearing New London Harbor, I feel boundaries

dissolve, and I'm the hundred tiny bells
the halyards clink on the sailboats at rest.
By the time night drops down its dull foil sheets,
by the time I enter the mouth of the river,
I am ocean and sky,
gull-bone and light,
I am salt. I am seasmoke.

PEMAQUID BEACH AFTER A WEEK ALONE

A man and a woman, not young,
are walking at tideline.
He wears a railroad cap pushed back,
his stomach presses against his jeans.
I can see the veins in her legs,
her blue blouse, the faded blossoms.

They walk as though it hurts a little to walk,
bent slightly forward,
an almost imperceptible limp.
Their hands are clasped, palms barely touching,
in the way of those who have held hands for years.
He stops to pick a seaweed-tangled rope
from the line of wrack,

pulls off bladder-wrack and kelp, rolls the rope
into a coil he will take home with him.
I envy them,
mooring-hitched to old love and the coastline.

The waves are pink combers
just touching the shore.
I've been sitting on a driftwood log
a long time, watching
one couple after another stroll down the beach
in this last grand light.

It seems to me they are an endless line in time,
moving forward toward me across the sand
toward the rocky point, then turning to walk back—
two by two.

ON HEARING OF THE SUDDEN
DEATH OF A FRIEND

The beach bristles with dead
and beautiful things:
slipper shells washed
full of sand,
broken blue mussels,
dried rockweed and kelp;
the sand itself, not the color
I think of when I say sand,
but specks: white finer
than salt, mica-shine,
dark brown,
pepper specks of black.
Beach plums line
the grassy path to the sea,
fuchsia and white,
full of show and radiance.
I've set a clam shell
on my writing table,
by the window
that looks over John's Bay.
In slow-time here,
I am learning to look closely.
The shell has a tiny hole in it,
is limed white as bone.
When someone dies,
where does all
that energy go?
Where does thought go
and attention?
Where does radiance go?
Three sailboats, anchored,
are rocking.
One fishing skiff, white, far off,
motors away from me.

Heat, enough of it that the yews
hiding the headstone raise a rash
on my arms as I pull them back.
Below, the Mississquoi River lifts
a languid brown body toward headwaters
where the blue herons breed.
No one else here on this unkept ground;
train tracks just beyond the boundary
are the only sign
that anyone's recently passed near.

Forty years, mother, and I drop to my knees—
with bare nails claw grass and sod
from the ground plate to free your initials,
struggle with thumb-thick branches.
I twist and tear them, scratching my arms,
hurl them to the ground.
Hot, drudging work—pain, a healing thing.

Such wildness here that I wonder
what lies beneath it, want to dig until I hold
in my arms what I lost as a child,
breast bone, pelvis, skull,
whatever might be left of you.
Instead I lug armloads of boughs to the weeds
beside the tracks, unload them heavily there.
An Amtrak clatters minutes or a lifetime by,
window after window—brief curious faces.

LAMENTATION

No one could bury you.
In the year of no snow—no softness—
the ground froze hard as a tomb.
You died in the season's deadlock.

In the year of no snow, no softness
until spring, you lay in the charnel house.
You died in the season's deadlock—
the grass grown brown and sleet-enameled.

Until spring, you lay in the charnel house—
the roses, winter-killed, earth solid with ice—
the grass grown brown and sleet-enameled.
Deer froze to stone on the mountain.

Earth solid with ice—the roses, winter-killed,
the ground froze hard as a tomb.
Deer froze to stone on the mountain—
no one, not anyone, could bury you.

LIGHTNING SPREADS OUT
ACROSS THE WATER

It was already too late
when the swimmers began
to wade through the heavy
water toward shore,
the cloud's black greatcoat
flinging across the sun,
forked bolts blitzing
the blind ground,
splits and cracks
going their own easiest way,
and with them, the woman
in the purple tank suit,
the boy with the water-wings,
one body then another.
And this is nothing about God
but how Stone Pond turned
at the height of the day
to flashpoint and fire
stalking across the water,
climbing the beach
among the screams
and the odor of burned skin
until twelve of them
curled lifeless on sand
or floated on the tipped
white caps of the surface,
and twenty-two more
walked into the rest
of their lives
knowing what waits
in the clouds to claim them
is random—
that nothing can stop it,
that afterwards the pond

smooths to a stillness
that gives back,
as though nothing could move it,
the vacant imponderable sky.

WATCHING LIGHT IN THE FIELD

It may be part water, part animal—
the light—the long flowing whole
of it, river-like, almost feline,
shedding night, moving silent
and inscrutable into the early morning,
drifting into the low fields,
gathering fullness, attaching itself
to thistle and sweetgrass,
the towering border trees,
inheriting their green wealth—
blooming as if this
were the only rightful occupation,
rising beyond itself, stretching out
to inhabit the whole landscape.
I think of illuminations, erasures,
how light informs us, is enough
to guide us. How too much
can cause blindness. I think of memory—
what is lost to us, what we desire.
By noon, nothing is exact,
everything diffused in the glare.
What cannot be seen intensifies:
rivulet of sweat across the cheekbone,
earthworm odor of soil and growing.
The field sways with confusion
of bird call, mewlings,
soft indecipherable mumblings.
But in the late afternoon, each stalk
and blade stands out so sharp and clear
I begin to know my place among them.
By sunset as it leaves—
gold-dusting the meadow-rue and hoary alyssum,
hauling its bronze cloak across the fences,
vaulting the triple-circumference
of hills—I am no longer lonely.

TWO

IN THE WINTER OF MY SIXTIETH YEAR

I

In the morning all things are released again
from the snow that sculpts the earth into its frozen self.
By the time the sun falls behind Daniel's Hill,
my hands will again know the shape of my face,
my legs will understand the weight of my body.
Then the night will erase it all again.
Each day, one more bed of intention; each night another erasure.

And what is the future—Vesuvius, the way it hunkers
over the village that has been buried seven times?
The mountain is quiet for now, but who knows?

There, somewhere in the long range of days behind me,
cameo carvers chiseled the faces of women
into orange shell carted from the Bay of Naples.
I was alive then.

And also on the Sunday in Chelsea
when a withered gypsy
told me falsehoods and the truth.

And alive also in the green land where
even the pasture-stones have names,
and all the names are incarnations of beauty.
If I don't tell them to you, you will imagine them
even more lovely then they are.

II

If I could find the wilding spirit
that used to animate my body,
with imagination this day could be anything,
and anyone could come into it.

The gypsy said: *You will go on three journeys.*

I have been on three journeys.

The gypsy said: *What is it you want?*
I want love to flow like sap through my veins,
I want a good wind to lift me beyond here;
I want to dance in the land of named stones.

And she said: *Is this really what you want?*

I am tired far beyond words.
I want to live in a cabin in the woods
and bake wheat loaves that rise
from the heat of the woodstove.

Do you want to live alone?

I have been alone
in this crack-cold landscape many seasons.
The icicles on my roof are long, and depend
toward a ground too slippery for my feet;
I keep counsel with myself and my old dog;
my bed is narrow with habit, wide with grief,
unfriendly to strangers.

WHEN I WAKE TO A BEDROOM FILLED
WITH BLUE LIGHTS

I open my eyes to a room sharp
with the dog's bark and blue
with the flashing announcement
that once again in the world something's not right.

What calls four cruisers to block off Beaver Street,
the small town side street so quiet, so late?
Someone's been stopped. Some fugitive?
Drunk or drugged? Or merely skidded off-track

the way last winter I fell and broke my wrist
on the path to my own garage—the kind of trip-up
that takes one instant of not watching
to change your life. Exactly the way

out of a sound sleep, this strobe-light blue pulls me
into the middle of someone else's predicament
so that I know again for sure
that even the deadbolt on the door and the weight

of two comforters can't shut out the danger.
And because I have to find out what's going on,
to make sure the cops have the lid on,
I get my uncle's World War I binoculars

and go stand in the bathtub, ridiculous
in my Grandma Moses gown, hair sticking up,
because the window over it has the best view,
but I can't make out why a small car

is slanted across the street, why three guys
in jeans are standing around while a couple of cops
run up and down, or why the houses across the way,
the whole neighborhood,

appears and disappears in the strobes.
And there are no guns drawn, no blood,
no shouts, no one trying to escape, so that finally
I decide it's nothing after all

and go back to broken sleep, where the room continues
to pulse with blue for hours, and I dream—
a ten-gallon aquarium—and I am a peacock-tailed guppy,
swimming back and forth through water's blue maze.

Nothing takes you where you want to go: the bus of a wrong shape
lets you off down the hill by a park where a man you don't know
is walking his dog. He asks you to sail the Caribbean and seems
disappointed when you say you don't have six thousand dollars.

Back in your apartment you learn there have been
six random murders in five days. You learn the class you wanted
on form is already full and your keys are lost. They are always lost
or mixed up or tangled. Nothing opens easily.

A bird on your side lawn is mortally injured and somehow
you are to blame. You lay it in the tall weeds
and go away. All day it flies
after you—you cannot save it or kill it.

Your work has grown to a thick stack and the hunchback poet
bends over it, encouraging you. She is kind but the children
are lost again and you must leave your work to find them.
It is your fault, always your fault.
They come home scratched, dirty, unforgiving.

At your aunt's cocktail party, you seduce a fox-haired sailor.
In someone else's bed, the two of you lie down
to consume yourselves like over-ripe pears.
Although he's been dead for years, your husband breaks
through the door, his voice and fist raised, a rifle in the car.

On the floor of the crowded state hospital
you try to carve out a place, a bed of straw.

The boxcar moves forward into the mist.
Because there is little hope,
you must take the crying toddler in your arms and heal him
with just the right words.

This is all you can do.
Almost every night there are rain storms;
on the worst nights, tornadoes. You close yourself
in a room with no windows and hang on
to a railing, a chair, whatever you can.

If only there were keys—or a credit card
with a workable number; if only you could complain
to someone who would listen.

WEED IN DROUGHT

Underfoot, in dooryards,
in gardens, purslane
takes hold and prospers—
even against the tenacity
of August light,
even against the last
lifting of moisture
from crumbling soil,
even when the brook
has given up its bullheads
and runs to nothing,
even when mudbeds
crack to gray powder,
even while dust collects
in silent spinning
dervishes of wind,
when thirst becomes
constant as breath
and water, the only word
worth saying—
even if stars should flake,
thin as cast-off skin
in night's crinkled parchment—
even if cemeteries were
the last land left inhabited.
purslane clings down
and will continue to cling
onto its own dry roots,
matted and circled,
refusing to die,
recreating itself
out of the least
seared bit,
prostrate but succulent,
leaves paddle-shaped

and still rowing
the five-petaled flower,
rosettes of yellow,
into each light-blinded morning.

LOCATION

Robin Williams, they say, has already checked out,
moved on—but here, at the tag-end of this small town's
week-long Big Deal, here on blocked-off Main Street,
here among the watching star-struck crowd, the trailers

of Tri-Star Pictures are still lined up curbside and humming,
the cameramen are still angling for shots, and I, unstar-struck
at the moment and pleased with my new curly-cut, am only trying
to walk home from the Main Salon, when I find myself

up against a barricade, the cop struggling to hold spectators
back. But nothing's been happening for minutes, only
the heaped-up leaves littering Central Square, blowing
around the painted-to-look-run-down gazebo, the cannon—
its fake rust. So I ask the cop can I cross? He says

if I go now I can. I squeeze through and stroll out in my
fleecy brown jacket, my wicked-good hairdo.
Suddenly a loudspeaker—Voice from Everywhere, Nowhere—
fills the sky booming: YOU—THE LADY IN THE BROWN JACKET.

THE LADY IN THE BROWN JACKET. A thousand eyes turn, I freeze
mid-street, fifty, overweight, scarlet, not knowing: forward?
back? And everyone, the cameras that are about to roll,
the lighting wizards, prop-people, the stuntman

driving the gray Toyota wagon that's about to careen
across the square, the kid that's about to dash across
in front of it, the ambulance that's about to
in just one second, tear screaming down Court Street, the extras

that are looters, the ones that are the itchy-scratchy homeless,
the ones that are about to run away from the wild animals,
everyone, the hundreds huddled in the cold waiting for
Something To Happen, the whole world that's about to be born,

stops dead in its tracks—for me.

IN THE BASEMENT OF
THE FIRST CHURCH

In the kitchen the woman who carries her clothes
in a shopping cart stirs soup, a rich mahogany
broth. It boils in the iron cauldron.
I have given her this job which she loves
for the way it lifts her into a person.

The people are gathering in the dining room—
straying in one by one out of the cold square,
dumping their frayed coats on a long table.
The other tables are set; the soup is ready.

But before we can serve, the Director begins
a speech about value and popularity.
He stands on a loft above us
where he cannot see the people
sitting expectantly at the long tables.

There has been a vote to decide who among us
is the most popular;
gold stars have been awarded.
He is announcing stars,
and he does this very slowly, beginning with one star

and working up to ten. The soup
is getting cold. The people are getting hungrier
and hungrier. He doesn't see their hunger.
Not the time, or the cold, or my voice
in his ear—can stop him.

Finally it is too late, and the cold useless soup
is removed and the people,
whose needs were so great,
file out, hunger filling their stomachs.

The Director, who sees none of this, goes on
with his endless words, while the cook—
who has become nothing again—
and the staff-people—who are again reminded

they are not worth anything—
gather in the kitchen
and fight like birds at a feeder
over the leftover loaves.

FROM THE BLUE ROOM AT THE COLONY

It is one of those middle days, where nothing is necessary,
but I've a compulsion to get things down and hold them:
a hollow wooden loon on a coffee table,
the twin crescent rolls of breakfast, light as last night's moon.

Dictation is the alphabet of light, a woman writes on her forearm.
I, myself, have encoded the notes of the air on napkins,
and have had hefty conversations with a man in a booth
at the Blue Benn Diner—thick words, and a slice of apple pie.

The journal of the days here might dissolve quickly
when I leave and never be remembered,
like old news going up in the library's fireplace,
taking with it the song of language I have been playing.

The man I was speaking of earlier sinks into the
leather chair. We read poems to each other.
I ask him if he believes
we can take our words with us undiminished.

For now, I want to drown out all life beyond here.
This stopping place astonishes and delights:
the phone in the closet, the playbills, the way every
new thing takes pleasure in the sheer unfolding of itself.

I want to bring it back to me—this space and time—
after I'm home again, call it back whenever I want to.
I will walk off with it, like the silent thief
who strides off with all the gold on the dresser.

These things I'll keep: stars shaking at the web
of tree branches, pans clattering in the kitchen,
late talk, the light of the woman downstairs
who writes all night—who can never sleep-—

and the church carillon next door which chimes
its Vespers each evening, the song lasting
long after the bells stop ringing.

You have to know where you're going-—
down the dead end road
by the Old First Congregational Church
and the plot's not clearly marked—
you find it by the tiny wooden sign
and the cement walk leading from the main path
to the grave. There's a stand
of snow-snapped birches and a slab of granite,
table-size, lying flat, embedded in the earth.
Downhill, a dozen yellow school buses rumble by.
From here, you can see all Bennington and beyond
to the mountains, brown still,
too soon in this cold spring for his early leaf—
its transient gold.
A bell rings somewhere.

Who knows what calling in myself
has called me here?
Next over, the Lathams' grave is a granite bench
as if they knew I'd need one. I sit,
surrounded by a swarm of tiny flies.
My shadow (or my shade?) sits before me
like a herald of things to come; her hair moves
in the slightest shift of wind.

A grave below tends
toward a red-bowed wreath, dried brown,
that leans against it.
How many buried with him?—his wife
and children, six in all,
and all but two dead before he was.
His epigraph—*I had a lover's quarrel with the world,*
and Elinor's—*Wing to wing and oar to oar.*
They must have held each other up. I check to see
what other mourner might be near
and finding none, step on the gravestone
and walk it slowly, with my eyes closed—

four strides exactly, and four strides back.
Old man, old quarreler,
I can hear you grumble under my feet—
understand—I've stood on you for years.

BOUNDARIES

All week I will be driving to the seminar
in Concord; all week I will be passing
a red-bearded construction worker
by the side of Route 9 in the 7 a.m. sun.
Light flares off the gold hair on his forearms;

red dust rises all around him.
They are building a new road,
and he holds a wooden pointer at the boundary
between the shoulder and the one passable lane.
He keeps cars going like cows through a chute.

He wears a yellow hard hat,
doesn't look up.
The next day he sits in the same position,
the same folding chair.
I begin to imagine he's been there all along

holding the pointer through the wide afternoon
letting dusk settle around his shoulders,
keeping it steady all night.
I wonder what he thinks about all day
in the clouds of exhaust, in the heat rising.

The following day, for miles past him
I construct him a life: a trailer,
wife bringing cornbread and beans to him,
a beer, maybe two, television to light
their evening, the bed moving under them.

At night in my dream he appears at my door
holding a bouquet of Joe-Pye-weed,
asking me to change his life.
Day in, day out, all that week I think about him—
while I'm walking the dog, weeding tomatoes.

He is the fixed point;
I am nothing to him
in the endless line of bumpers passing.
Today, certain I'm invisible,
I drive past a last time. He is standing

watching the bulldozer roll the earth over
but suddenly he turns—and against the blur
of dust lifting and sun falling
in rivers of light through the trees,
he looks up—he waves at me.

I keep the intimacy of that instant,
past mile markers, past the low marsh,
past the dark grove of white pine,
past milkweed releasing froth to the wind,
toward the lucent black eye of a pond.

WINTER SKY OVER CHESHIRE COUNTY, NEW HAMPSHIRE

You are all blue-bruise and magenta where clouds hunch
like shoulders above the mahogany tree-trunks.
Above them, you fly up, dove-gray for miles.
All day I've watched you transmute:
lemon, nativity blue, flesh of the broiled salmon.
All day you shapeshift: buffing-cloth, rock-field,
ocean roiling spit and spume.
I would paint you
if you could stop, stay pinned on the canvas of my eye.
But you are a wily fellow—you leap up, the wind
takes you, the turning earth takes you. Oh you are
breath of ginger, cardamom, peppermint.
You smooth my forehead with a dew-moistened glove; rub up
against my hips and thighs. You ring like a church bell,
clang two spoons together, bang pans and dance.
To keep you, I swallow you whole; my abdomen swells
with your thousand colors—
all my cells explode with your light.

STARRY NIGHT

It was all gold swirl and indigo,
the way the heavens looked
with my head bent back to vertigo,
my hands loose at my side, palms turned up,
feeling the night sky
suffuse my entire body as I stood in my backyard,
in Keene, New Hampshire ,
beside the dark garden with its tall delphiniums.

And Van Gogh stood beside me, not mad entirely,
but capable of seeing with his skin,
his fingers, teaching me
to see the way he saw,
asking the questions I've asked,
responding with images as distant and encompassing
as the night fires
that spun their old spirals above the landscape

in that place where time became all one moment,
so that the French town we stood in
(Saint Remy was it?)
was only a silhouette beyond the guarding cypress,
except for the dozen houselights that persisted—
little dabs of light that illumined
only their own small spaces
and might wink out at any moment.

FALL GARDEN AND THE WEATHER COMING IN

Vines cramp around each other
and blanch fever-pale.

Late tomatoes refuse to open
their green fists

and the squash leaves lie conquered
by their own multiplication. The soil stiffens.

Even the insects have taken leave
of their abbreviated lives.

Two crows flap in the butternut tree.
Leaves spin a yellow shower through the gray.

What golem raises up in the garden's
dust-devil, clambers over the hedges?

I've no voice for it.
What is it I cannot say?

If but those crows, their minimal alarms,
were the only ruckus in this world.

INVOCATION

You came to me first as dawn hauled up on ropes
of apricot above the blackened wall of white pine.

You came from the south, from the highest places,
came down the mountain running.

You were announced by the crows, the shrill
calls of alarm from the uppermost branches.

You opened your throats in a high harsh singing.
I didn't know what you were and rose trembling

from the deck chair, stood breathless and still
where the woods surrounded me, gathered dark

and darker as if to stall the light.
You came down, two of you: one young and red-bright

the other old, rust streaked with gray.
You pretended not to know me and lay down

beneath a small granite ledge, lay on the fallen
needles, licking light into your fur.

You came to me because I have wanted you.
You came though I had asked for nothing,

because I was full as a river at flood tide
with sadness.

You came to me, rested and then rose, first one,
then the other, and ran downhill into the morning.

You who assumed the guise of foxes, come again
as you did that morning on the mountainside.

And wasn't that you who came last summer
as whale boiling up from the waters of Jeffries Shoal?

Wasn't it you who came in September as wood duck
over the Stoddard marshes, who flew parallel to my car window?

Come to me again as moose invisible on the night road.
Come the way deer steal across the field at dusk.

Come as raccoon, as coyote. Come carrying your burden
of blood and shadow—

come joyous and light with song, come in sleep,
in the unexpected reaches of the day. I am waiting.

Come red-tailed or black-winged; come fluked
and finned, come clawed and taloned,

renew my breath, come full of the mystery
I am only beginning to know.

THE READING: UNIVERSITY COLLEGE, GALWAY

The sound beyond the dining hall windows
began at the edge
of our consciousness, then rose
until we could no longer ignore it.
It drew our attention
beyond the resounding voice of the poet
to a strange and strident music
that filled the twilight sky just beyond
the thick stone walls—
a mingled cacophony of sound
halting the poet finally, mid-way in his poem,
so that he looked up astonished.
And we all looked up
at the high clerestory windows—
in which the crows,
black silhouettes, winged past by the hundreds,
thousands, waves of them, an entire river,
as if a film about portents rolled by the windows,
ceaselessly past, and we sat, transfixed, listening.
It was as if the Irish sea
clattered all its shells together, or the stone walls
of Inishmore turned to metal and fell,
with a rusty cranking, all at once to the stone land,
the sky cackling, cawing, shrieking, pieces of it moving—
as if all the ghosts of Ireland flew
in an uproar,
heckling, cantankerous,
as if all the kings and legends of Ireland
streamed there.
After the window-glass showed nothing
but the darkening blue-violet of the sky,
and the clamor diminished until it was only
a distant chorus from the nearby grove,
the poet continued,

his voice as thunderous as before,
his body leaning into his words,
his hands marking time to his meters.
But we were no longer with him,
having taken flight beyond the room
into some world of faerie, daemon, elemental language.

NEAR GALWAY

The monk (I thought he was a monk),
came through the two-acre grove,
down the path in his brown robe,
cord knotted at his waist.
I saw him from the corner of my eye.

And I might have dropped back
and let him catch up. I might have spoken
but for the warning sign at the head of the path—
the sign that said in tall black:
Don't walk after dark alone.

And in *any* case, I might have spoken—
the night an hour away after all
and him, a monk, and the grove so small
(though hung with shadow and the clamor
of blackbirds in the oaks).

I might have asked him: *What is your life?*
But the dark was coming, and I thought
of other paths, other men, and other warnings—
so the moment went past,
and he followed behind me,

far behind, not walking fast.
And I went on alone
through the bars of the trees
and came out in the light.
And out of my fear, we did *not* speak.

DUBLIN BEGGAR

In the courtyard of St. Teresa of Avila's, just before mass,
she sprawled on the stones,
her back against the building,
a thicket of black hair tangling across her face.
Her age was unknowable—
but nearly old—as I am nearly old,
skirts spread in billows around her like shadow.
I leaned down and touched her.
No, I leaned on the church wall and watched her.
No.

She made me sad and terrified.
You know how it is—
you don't know what helps and what doesn't.
You want to be good.
You want to walk away and not think about it.
I walked half a block beyond her, then turned
and went back.

As I dug through my change-purse for coins,
I tried to look into her ruined face;
she didn't look at me—there was no sign that she saw me—
No sign she saw anything,
her black eyes focused on nothing,
or on something far off beyond the high wall.

How can the spirit fall from the body—
who allows it and where does it go?
No one can carry it back after it's gone too far.
Beyond us, three tolls of the church bell,
and the tuppence, the twenty pence,
I tossed into the black hat
turned upside-down on the walk
made no sound when they fell.

PILOT GLASSES

When I put them on the sky turned bluer than it was,
and the hills, as if suffused with gold, glowed
like an Old Master's oil.

*

We were driving back from Montpelier where we met our
California e-mail friends. It was the first time I'd seen them in their
real bodies, instead of the bodies of words lofted across a continent.
I knew them and didn't know them. What is added when we see a
thing we have only touched with language? Patrick handed his
glasses to me.

I put them on,
and in those tinted lens,
the mountains turned to topaz, emerald, garnet.

*

Once, at my old job in an ugly city, the receptionist came back from
the cellar where she'd gone to store files. Talking high and fast, she
said she'd looked through the basement window into the storm
drain outside, which was covered at ground level with an iron grill.
At the bottom of the drain, lying there, was an impossible animal:
two-headed, pink and beige. We didn't, of course, believe her.

One after another, we went down
into that place of moldy dampness,
into the dust.
But each returned
with the same strange story:
two heads, pink and beige.
I was last.

I went down into the
dust and dim, and found my way
to the window that was the one light,
and looked through it.

And looked again.
In truth,
the creature was pink fur and beige fur.
It had two heads
and both were sleeping.

*

What is it we see when we see?
Whatever held me to that perception
lifted, and I saw
not one, but two of them, one tan—one white,
their small tails curled around their small bodies—
tame creatures whose gone-wild mother
had gone off and left them,
lying one across the back of the other,
asleep and unaware.

What is it we want to see?
Patrick said I looked good in the glasses.
I kept them on for a long time
as the Green Mountain autumn
flew, heightened and sharp-edged, by us,
and the sky with its brilliant and irregular
triangles of turquoise stayed steady
between the clouds. That illusion—I held
on to it for a long time,
because there was nothing confusing then—
nothing that was not beautiful.

ROOFMEN

Over my head, the roofmen are banging shingles into place
and over them the sky shines with a light that is
almost past autumn, and bright as copper foil.

In the end, I will have something to show for their hard labor—
unflappable shingles, dry ceilings, one more measure of things
held safely in a world where safety is impossible.

In another state, a friend tries to keep on living
though his arteries are clogged,
though the operation left a ten-inch scar

and, near his intestines, an aneurysm blossoms
like a deformed flower. His knees and feet
burn with constant pain.

We go on. I don't know how sometimes.
For a living, I listen eight hours a day to the voices
of the anxious and the sad. I watch their beautiful faces

for some sign that life is more than disaster—
it is always there, the spirit behind the suffering,
the small light that gathers the soul and holds it

beyond the sacrifices of the body. Necessary light.
I bend toward it and blow gently.
And those hammerers above me bend into the dailiness

of their labor, beneath concentric circles: a roof of sky,
beneath the roof of the universe,
beneath what vaults over it.

And don't those journeymen
hold a piece of the answer—the way they go on
laying one gray speckled square after another,

nailing each down, firmly, securely.

NAMING

Don't say love	Don't say dreams
say land	say ocean
say rock and soil	say water and salt

no, don't say that

say igneous rock and acid soil	say saline water and seasalt
say gray and brown	say green and slate
or red clay and ochre desert	or indigo deep and turquoise shallow
say hard thing and soft thing	say wet thing and sliding thing

of the earth

say little pebble, say finest dust	say smallest drop, say little ripple
say barn and building built upon	say cave and cavern swimming within
say car and train riding on it	say boat and iceberg riding on it

no, don't say that

say sedan stopping	say sailboat tacking
say freight train	say ice pinnacle

riding on

say man and woman and animal	say fish and seaweed and whale
living there and within	living under and within

no, don't say that

say greyhound and koala bear	say pilot fish, rockweed, orca
say man in tweed Irish cap	say merman hiding beneath a ledge
say woman whose hair falls forward	say silkie singing her endless notes
her breath rising, whose arms	as she swims across the sea
are muscled with long pulling	across the deep troughs of the water
say someone loves	say someone dreams

no, don't say that

say a man brings pasture roses	say a woman is drifting beneath Orion
say someone holds someone	say someone's head is on the pillow
a long time,	and their sleep is filled with gods,
and the darkness goes away	and the darkness goes away.

ANNIVERSARIES
for Donald Sheehan

This is the day of Hiroshima,
the flashpoint day of bodies, bright
as the briefest star. And you remind me
that this day is also a high holy day,
the transfiguration, when Christ went up
on the mountain and in the company of three
disciples, became light just as those
Japanese bodies became light.

I am sitting on a gray folding chair
thinking about connections—August 6th,
my God—the day my father died. Not moving,
not taking my eyes from the compassion
in your face, I stumble back to my tenth summer,
the phone call that blasted something away forever.
Suicide leaves survivors wanting something
to explain it, the way even now I want
some cloaked guide to step from the shadow
of a casket saying: *This, child, is how it was.*

Noontime, on the gentle slope of lawn,
a woman tells me on this day
last year, she set flowers and candles
adrift on a long river for the world.
And I wonder how, against the immensity
of Christ or of arms, incandescent in a cruel
cloud, one small death can matter,
can share the same syllables in the throat,
the same vowels floating across the vaporous air.
My father. My father.

Later, from one small bedroom window,
I watch the soft arching of Mt. Kinsman,
a blue sky and a cloud rising,
a lightning rod atop a cupola.
The day gathers itself: this festival,
Hiroshima, these hills, your voice,

and yes, Christ, in whom I may not even believe,
and the suicide of my father, all lifting
into this pine-laden air, all rising
and igniting like candles,
like a procession of flowers and candles
over these wavering White Mountains.

The Frost Place, Franconia, New Hampshire

STILL WATER

. . . what times are these when a poem about trees is almost a crime because it contains silence against so many outrages.

—Bertolt Brecht

And why not silence?
Ahead of me, Goose Pond parts pale water
and my canoe slides through into June sun, cathedral quiet,
                              soft plums of cloud.
A thin gauze of rain stalls over Mt. Monadnock.

This is the way I drift

from each skirmish with the world
to the diplomacy of light
as it flares off the water,
                              flickers among the flute-notes
of birds hidden in the leaning birches.

Would you condemn me?

I've already held the old bodies of grief
long past morning; leave them
to the ministrations
                              of the dirt-borers
who work what is finished back into the earth.

Some atrocities are beyond redemption—

you know them already—
the world will be the world no matter.
I want the blinding silver of this small pond
                              to stun my eyes,
the palaver of leaves to stop my ears.

Today in a meadow beside the sea
I knelt among sea rocket and lupine
as a deer I'd startled flipped heels up
and bounded into the spruce grove.
Prebbles Cove, the beach of stones
glistening and smooth from the pummel of waves.
And I, who understand pounding,
wanted to walk into the sea, to rock there.

At the far edge of my life
on an island four hundred miles
from home, I lean against
an uncurtained window, and all my grief
for what is already lost,
for what it may be too late to find,
jostles up against how much
I continue anyway to love the world.

I am tired of wanting to sleep beyond waking—
tired of the numbing that is no better than death.
But here on the sill, stones oval as eggs—
blue, gray, black, a whole row of them—
glow in the afternoon light
and here, across the meadow,
light enfolds even the least
small running creature.

And here. And here. And here.
More light, great sheets of saving light
surge and flash—green, coral, cerulean—
off the turbulent
white-capped waters.

ACKNOWLEDGMENTS

GRATEFUL ACKNOWLEDGMENT IS MADE TO THE EDITORS OF THE publications in which the following poems first appeared:

"Gifts" in *Ad Hoc Monadnock: an Anthology*; "Lamentation" and "The Decision" in *Calliope*; "Anniversaries" in *Kalliope*; "At the Enosberg Falls Cemetery" and "Sag Harbor at Sundown" in *The Laurel Review*, "Crossing the Sound" in *Mankato Poetry Review*; "Weed in Drought" in *The Midwest Quarterly*; "Invocation" in *Ploughshares;* "Going" and "Pemaquid Beach After a Week Alone" in *Poet Lore*; "Still Water" in *Poetry;* "In the City Without a Name," "Location," and "First Church Basement" in *Poetry Northwest;* "Evensong" in *Sou'Wester;* "Breaking Silence—for My Son" in *The Spoon River Poetry Review;* "From Eleven Years Later" in *Zone 3.*

"Visiting Frost's Grave" won the 1997 Robert Frost Poetry Award sponsored by the Robert Frost Foundation in Lowell, Massachusetts.

Many thanks to the MacDowell Colony and the Dorset Writer's Colony, where some of these poems were written. And special thanks to my writing friends for the gift of their critiques and their friendship, to Brendan Galvin who, so many years ago, set me on this road, and to Mary Oliver for her support and encouragement.

ABOUT THE AUTHOR

PATRICIA FARGNOLI HOLDS A BACHELOR OF ARTS FROM TRINITY College in Hartford and a Master of Social Work from the University of Connecticut. A longtime resident of Windsor, Connecticut, Pat has for the last five years made her home in Keene, New Hampshire. In 1998, she retired from her career as a clinical social worker and psychotherapist to devote her time to teaching at the Keene Institute of Music and Related Arts and writing poetry.

In the spring of 1998, she was awarded a fellowship at the MacDowell Colony, and she has been in residence several times at the Dorset Writer's Colony in Dorset, Vermont. She has published widely in such literary journals as *Poetry, Ploughshares, Prairie Schooner, Poetry Northwest, The Laurel Review* and *The Indiana Review*. She was the recipient of the 1997 Robert Frost Literary Award and has received several other awards for her poetry.

She has three adult children and two grandchildren.

THE MAY SWENSON POETRY AWARD

THE MAY SWENSON POETRY AWARD WAS NAMED FOR MAY Swenson, and honors her as one of America's most provocative, insouciant, and vital poets. During her long career, May published eleven volumes of poems, and she was loved and praised by writers from virtually every major school of poetry. She left a legacy of nearly fifty years of writing when she died in 1989.

May Swenson lived most of her adult life in New York City, the center of poetry writing and publishing in her day. But she is buried in Logan, Utah, her birthplace and hometown.

SEP 5 2000